Associates that helped me make this book,

Sandy Leipold

Patricia Young

Cheryl Brewer

Ken Piercy

Teresa Brewer

Gina Brewer

Lisa Seabeck

Poetry
at Its Best

Berniece Piercy

authorHOUSE®

AuthorHouse™
1663 Liberty Drive
Bloomington, IN 47403
www.authorhouse.com
Phone: 1 (800) 839-8640

Published by AuthorHouse   07/28/2017

ISBN: 978-1-5246-9477-7 (sc)
ISBN: 978-1-5246-9476-0 (e)

Print information available on the last page.

Any people depicted in stock imagery provided by Thinkstock are models,
and such images are being used for illustrative purposes only.
Certain stock imagery © Thinkstock.

This book is printed on acid-free paper.

Contents

Highest Goals From Heaven

The highest goals we seek, are surely made in heaven.
It could be a challenge, these goals are
not always so easy to acquire.

Keep on trying, do your best, even if you fail at first,
You will see a difference, you will know,
how strong you really are.

No one who has already won, ever said
that winning would be easy.
You have to dream of winning, and
always keep a hopeful heart.

Just pray each day, and God will help you with this mission.
You will rejoice in your victory, that was
possible with God, right from the start.

Written By
Berniece Piercy
2008

Precious Hours

I hold this child within my arms
This lovely angel one,
To soothe a hurt or gently rock,
So spent and tired when day is done,

The lovely curls upon thy brow,
Thy face with pure content,
I feel such love within my heart,
Such innocence that God has sent,

It seems like only hours ago,
You ran from place to place,
Such fibrant energy so strong,
With a never ending pace,

With toys and make_believe, so true
You've traveled miles so wide,
The moon, the stars, the days of old,
You laughed alot, and ran and cried,

So rest my tiny one in peace,
In dreams of purest gold,
I'll hold you safe within my arms,
Until the evening hours are old,

My love will always ever be, a special
Part of you, my dear,
For God will hold us close, my love,
As He is ever oh, so near.

By Berniece Piercy

Autumns Magic

A burst of golden reddish hue,
Across the countryside,
As autumn accents skies of blue,
The beauty splashes so far and wide,

A touch of sadness fills my heart,
That this will have to end,
Impressions of the finest art,
Unto my mind, this scene does lend,

Autumn holds so many dreams,
For young and old, you know,
Of days where thoughts of love it seems,
Make many fond affections grow,

A smokey haze thats everywhere,
The scent of burning leaves,
Togetherness, someone to care,
September, thus, it's magic weaves,

A carpet soft, beneath my feet,
Where many leaves did fall,
In eagerness each day I meet,
As autumn captures us, one and all.

By Berniece Piercy

Family Life

The days of family life are rare, it seems, the
love that we knew just isn't there anymore,
It takes a special kind of loving care, and truest
feelings, must be, really sincere, as it was before,

It's very sad, when fading love does happen, for
everyone will have to pay the highest price, someday,
When nothing even matters anymore, then all mankind
just loses touch, and no one really has anything nice to say,

When our brothers and sisters are split, so far apart,
and the parents are seeing their children go astray,
There is no way to reach them, as they slip and slide
in life, and finally each one just goes a separate way,

The hearts are broken and bleeding, with no
love or joy in their lives, it will never be,
And one day they will all cry out, please love me, but
there will be no one to listen, or anyone to see,

Yes, Jesus will be watching over everything, He
knows that so many have already lost their way,
He will listen to everyone, if they will just take
the time to talk to Him each passing day,

Oh, for the comfort and closeness, and the family warmth
again, the truest love that is waiting, as it grows old,
It could be that one day, it may be too late, and
the words of lost love can never be told.

By Berniece Piercy

I Am Your Flag

I am your flag, don't trod on me,
I have flown for peace, thru all history,
And wars were fought, and lives were lost,
And I still fly today, at a tremendous cost.

For cannons have roared, and planes have dived low,
And the sky was filled, with an orangish glow,
All the dust and the smoke, and the cries of great pain,
And the cold, cold ground, yes, we were at war again.

All the battles were won, with the strength that God gave,
And my red, white, and blue image,
in the winds it did wave,
No matter the foe, how big or how strong,
We will fight to the end, tho the battles may be long.

Don't trod on me, I am so proud to fly,
For each stripe and each star is for
liberty, and the right to try,
America gives us the right to dream, and
if we are weary a place to rest,
Where justice rules, and our lives will be best.

Hold your head high, oh, so proud you should be,
For you are an American, I know you can see,
As long as I fly over America, the peace will stay,
And I will always try, with God's help, to keep it that way.

"A haven of freedom" is called America, I
will watch over each peaceful shore,
I am your flag, be proud, yes, I will fly
over America, forevermore.

Written by Berniece Piercy
Written October 1993

Winter Magic

The rustle of the tumbling leaves, as the breeze sweeps clean
the walk,
And winter whispers with each gust, of cold and snowy talk,
As you know the icy pattern, that shuts us in each year,
It will be such a long time, until springtime months appear.

Still the castles are so beautiful, in the mounds of whitest
winter snow,
And the twinkle, lacy snowflakes, all the loveliest designs
they show,
As the logs burn in the fireplace, and the shadows slowly
creep,
How the flames dance, oh, so wildly, on the crackling red hot
coals, they leap.

Summer cannot know this special magic, being with you so
snug and warm,
While winter shows it frantic fury, then spent, so quietly,
lends it's charm,

I guess we really must confess, we don't know what we want,
it's true,
The very best of the four seasons, is the beauty of each day
with you.

Berniece Piercy

When Life Was Young

So soon forgotten childhood days,
When the tide of life comes in,
All the laughter and the merriment,
As the simple ways of life begin,

For the twinkle of the bluest eyes,
Or a little curly locks next door,
Our truest friend for all our life,
We never needed one thing more,

How far away, how faded now,
How trodden down into the earth,
As mile, and many miles again,
Have come and gone, since first our birth

If I could turn back time once more,
To a quiet, happy yesterday,
When life was young and gentle,
When we were children at our play.

Written
1983
By Berniece Piercy

Winter Wonderland

When I looked out my window,
At the winter wonderland,
I knew this lovely scenery,
Was painted by God's hand,
The trees were dressed in lacy gown,
So picture perfect to the eye,
Surrounded by the peaceful town,
A part of winter's delightful lullaby,
I looked beyond the meadow,
Undisturbed under a blanket of white,
Mother Nature's flowers and greenery,
Were sleeping beneath the earth,
And hidden from my sight,
When the sunshine comes in early spring,
Melting furrows in the mounds of snow,
I know that winter time will warm, and go away,
It will return next year, with much beauty, this I know.

Berniece G. Piercy

Wasted Years

I am looking at so many wasted years, special times that came
   and died along the way,
A river that is filled with hopeless tears, how could we have
   thrown away, even a single day?

Love has escaped so many persons, it is true, a coldness in
This world has come to take it's place,
No one stops to see the lovely flowers, or the sky so blue, the
World is turning and moving, at an unbelievable pace,

The only thing that can happen to this earth, that is so lost,
Is for Jesus to come and help us, and save everyone,
Loving and caring have been given up at such a terrible cost,
We must embrace the love that we can find each day, or soon
   it may all be wasted, and forever gone.

Written
2007
By Berniece Piercy

You Can Do It

You know you can do it,
It just takes some sweat and tears.
They say, anything is possible,
Even if we have try for years.

Do you have the self control?
And can you stand the rigid rules?
Do you have the confidence?
The faith, the hope, you'll need these tools.

"I cant', the words that will end it all,
It's true, that's the easy way to go.
But you will never meet the challenge,
And the sweet success, you will never know.

Ask God up above to help you,
But you must also try it on your own.
Be happy at what you are doing.
You are not out there standing alone.

The glory and fame of just winning,
And knowing you did it all.
Will light up your life, and suddenly,
You will be standing so very tall.

Written by Bernice Piercy

Truest Love

As I sit here by my window, and I look beyound the gate,
Then I rock the chair so gently, time has passed, and the
Afternoon grows late.
If I could see your dear, sweet face, and it would come to me,
Once again,
If my hand could touch and soothe your brow, to take away your
Forever pain.
My arms are now so empty, and my heart is heavy so,
You will always be my own sweet love, a part of me will be
with you, Wherever you may go.
Now as the time just slips away, and still I see, you are not going
To be there,
I sit and wait, the hours pass, I prey that you will not forget me,
And that you really do care.
Seems I have grown so much older now, and wiser yes, this
I know,
For wishing does not make it happen, nor can I stop, the rushing
River's flow.
But if a love, so strong and true, can last a lifetime through,
I'll stay right here, and dream again, and wait until I see, my
precious you.

Berniece Piercy

The Smallest Treasure

Although you're just a tiny flower,
In a forest, dark and deep.
Where stillness does surround you,
And it seems that all is fast asleep.

You do add a special beauty,
Tho small and trodden down.
You must stand tall and stately,
In your lovely, purple colored gown.

For you are truly chosen,
To always play a part,
Of making life so beautiful,
From the moment, time did start.

I can't imagine living,
In a world all brown and gray.
I have the greatest need for you,
And I hope that you will always stay.

Written By
Berniece Piercy
1985

The Longest Journey

We have cut so many trails in life's old weathered hide.
Always searching for new horizons, near
and far, across the countryside,
We have to stop and plant some roots,
someplace, sometime in our life, they say,
Have to find someone to love us, give us
peace and happiness along the way,
We have to win so many battles; have
to lose some of them too,
We must change some of our lifestyles;
learn to venture to the new,
Climb the mountains, cross the desert;
span the ocean, reaching far,
Learn the ways of famous persons, and
be tall enough to touch a star,
Then maybe one day, years from one, someone will
pass close by, and say, this was a special person,
who conquered life, in his or her own way.

By Berniece Piercy
2003

The Peace And Love Of Christmas

Remember a happy Christmas Eve, when our
loved ones helped to decorate the tree.
There was closeness for everyone, a stolen kiss under
the mistletoe, a special hug for you and me.

With the garland and tinsel, and candy canes,
delicate ornaments, to carefully hang once more.
We wanted everything to be perfect, bringing back
images of how our Christmas day was before.

What a beautiful tree with the twinkling bulbs,
when the lights were turned down low.
Folks gathered to sing Christmas carols, and
holiday reflections outside in the snow.

The stockings were hung by the fireplace,
waiting for Santa to call.
A golden angel so high, at the top of
the tree, to oversee it all.

For Christmas dinner we were all together, we had
the love, the laughter, and the happiness that day.
So many years of treasured memories, so much we
wanted to do, and the loving words we wanted to say.

Our dear ones wanted to stay here with us, but the angels
came to take them home to heaven, and we miss them so.
They are loved and happy with Jesus, but they
are also here with us today, we know.

The beautiful moments that won't be forgotten, a close
embrace, a loving glance, a smile that will always stay.
Engraved in the book of our lives, we will keep in our
hearts, with all the love we knew, along life's way.

Now, as we celebrate the birth of Jesus, with a
Christmas tree, our family dinner, presents to
exchange, and songs to sing, there will be peace
and love for everyone, that will always last.
But it will never replace the yesterdays, that held
us all together, on each beautiful Christmas day,
the forever memories, that remind us always, of the
precious years, with our loved ones, from the past.

Written By
Berniece Piercy
2008

The Cost of Freedom

Our hearts ache for all the young boys,
Who must leave and go to war,
They are hardly more than children,
Sent to lands across the sea, afar.

Tho each Mother's tears are falling,
Thoughts are troubled, times are sad,
Yes, each Father's pride is hailing,
This is their son, this handsome lad.

Young in face and young in spirit,
And oh, so young in manly ways,
Thrown into all of the brutality,
Where death conquers, where death lays.

This boy will fight for our great country,
Till the end, if it need be,
So everyone can live in freedom,
We will not give it up, you see.

Still memories echo of the children,
Playing soldier, set to win,
With their toy guns, they ran, they hid,
They liked the game, they played again.

But war is hell, and it is real,
They can't throw down their guns and quit,
Can't close their eyes, and it will go,
Cannot escape the force of it.

Friends they've known, and war time buddies,
Comrades falling, where they will lie,
Some are bleeding, and hurt so badly,
Some won't make it, they'll watch them die.

As tears spring forth, "Oh, God, have mercy",
The task of war, the awful cold,
These boys have only empty feelings,
And suddenly, they've grown so old.

They long to leave this all behind them,
And Home does seem so far away,
"Oh, Mom and Dad, and Sis and Brother,
I pray I'm coming Home to stay."

Berniece G. Piercy

The First Step

First I know, that I must walk, before I ever learn to run,
This will be difficult for me, to start life, as if it had just begun,

I hope the strength I need is there, as each slow and painful
step I take,
At day's end, tho weary I may be, I will feel brand new, when
I awake,

I will reach out and truly find, the helping hand that I will need,
And new dreams will surround me so, I will grow and prosper
from life's seed,

For Jesus will be watching me, as I face each given day,
Yes, I have needed all his help, to bring me peace along
life's way,

So, may I do my very best, to be strong, and forward go,
And always give thanks to Jesus, who has given me the love,
that I need to grow.

Written
1980
By Berniece Piercy

To Catch a Tear

When someone's heart is hurting, and you reach out your
    hand to them, to catch a tear,
God is there to see your compassion, He will reward your
    kindness someday, or some year,

God's love is always waiting there, He knows us well, He
    oversees our daily deeds,
Only we can prove our goodness, as we pray to God, and
    follow Jesus, wherever He leads,

It is such a little thing to reach out your hand, and lift
    someone up,
For they need help, no matter what their many reasons,
Only God can judge our choices, as we live on, and travel
    thur life's seasons,

Look up to the sky, and smile, for you can see the sun,
Your heart is pure, you've done the best you can, each day,
To show your love to everyone you meet, who struggles
    endlessly,
You know, Jesus has truest love, that can save them, He alone
    can show them all, the chosen way.

Written
Spring 2006
By Berniece Piercy

The Ways Of The Lord

The ways of the Lord, are gentle,
And yes he understands our plight,
His love is so very rewarding,
From each new dawn, until the ending night.

The ways of the Lord are waiting,
For the souls that are weary and lost,
As they finally return from the wasted trails,
Of heartache and misery, and paying the cost.

As Jesus will take each unto him,
Every moment becomes so peaceful and calm,
Then everyone can really understand,
The beautiful words of the twenty third psalm.

Written By
Berniece Piercy
1975

This Peaceful Resting Place

The many flags that adorn this peaceful resting place,
Are moving gently in the softest breeze today,
They are a symbol of the bravery, of the lives they gave,
For their country, on this saddest Memorial Day,

I am looking over the many surrounding flags, that represent
    America's Armed Forces,
As we stand in the glowing sunshine's warmth that we all know
There are so many loved ones, crying, close beside me
In the quiet reverence that they show,

We are remembering all the yesterdays, the special times,
That bring the many treasured thoughts to mind,
Now, the years will pass, life will go on, and time will ease this
    reality is here today,
Yes, we will come back here once again, over and over,
To feel the loving closeness to you, that we will find,

And when we walk away, we will have known, the feeling of
    love, in this beautiful sacred place,
This haven of closeness, where God surrounds you so,
We know you are safe here, in His arms, with all His loving grace,

And we thank Him for all the precious years, that He gifted
     us, with you in our lives,
We miss you so much, as we face each new tomorrow,
We will live in the light of the blessings, that God gives,

Memorial Day
1980's
By Berniece G. Piercy

The Candle Of Hope

The candle of hope is still flickering in the wind, for there
is still strength and faith, to get us through the night.
Perhaps the love and the good feelings that we have,
Will bring forth a new tomorrow, and
everything will be all right.

We have reached out to touch the edge of destiny,
Not knowing what we will meet that
will stop us, along the way.
It can be wonderful and bursting with much happiness,
As God surrounds us, and protects us day by day.

We know God's purpose for us, here on earth.
We will always be part of his everlasting plan,
WE must go forth, and tell the people that we meet,
About God's love, and touch the lives of everyone we can.

The candle of hope will forever keep its brilliance,
And all will be following this light that shines afar.
When hope is fading, and panic comes
your way, grab someone's hand,
And be united, together we can reach that brightest star.

Written By Berniece Piercy
2006

Searching

Please help me as I take one step, for I greatly
Fear I will fall,
I'm trying with my very soul, my best to give my all.
May I touch so gently, your life, your heart, your
Mind.
All of your time I will not occupy, but for
The briefest moment, may I find,
The feelings that we all search for, and for the
Goodness in our lives,
The faith, the hope, the kindness, all of the
Things in life, for which man strives.
Perhaps if in this lifetime, I am blessed
In this special way,
I will keep this glow of sunshine, to give back
To you again, someday.

Written: 2001
By Berniece Piercy

Portions of Love

A little bit of love can go a long, long way,
And the smallest prayer will really show we care,
Each smile we meet, can help to make us happy,
As it sparkles like a diamond, oh, so rare,

Every bit of hope can make us feel much stronger,
And faith in God will sustain us thru each trying time,
The smallest goal, will count as one step forward,
And even nothing, can become a moment prime,

Each success will add up to a greatness,
Perhaps each dream, can someday be a reality,
When we have touched a star, there will be no turning back,
All of this one day, will make our life a specialty,

If we have love for Jesus, and the whole wide world,
Without asking for anything in return, each coming day,
God will reward us, our lives will be as rich as gold,
Because we gave our love to all, and we walked with Jesus,
    all the way.

Written
2007
Berniece G. Piercy

Our Home

This home is big and sprawling,
And yes, silence is the king,
No little voices do I hear,
No happy times, no anything.

No family lives here, anymore,
And soon its emptiness will show,
All lives will change and hearts will cry.
And this hurt inside will never go.

You cannot have what isn't there,
And wishes are not always true,
But life will go on, in spite of pain,
And this empty house will always bring
Precious memories to me and you.

Bernice Piercy
Written in the Summer 2000

My Children

Sometime in your hurried lives, just come my way,
And talk to me.
The days that pass, are much the same, I hardly hear from
Anyone, what a lonely life, this seems to be.

I am forever talking to the wind, or
praying to my God above,
I keep wishing you all, much happiness, and new hope for
You're tomorrow, with my unending love.

There are times I feel an inward pain, for I can't change,
This world at all.
Then I pray that God is beside me, and that He
Will always be there.
I am tired now, life's heavy load does bend me low,
But I know that God can lift me up, and take me anywhere.

I will always need His strength and love, His faith and hope,
And peaceful hours each coming day,
The sunshine bright, the robins song, the I can make it,
And survive and go on my way.

But, still I love to see you all, to give you a hug, and
Hold you oh, so tight,
And I do dream a bit of happy days gone by, and I know
That God can make everything in
our lives turn out all right.

Written: 1995
By Berniece Piercy

My Special Angel

This lady, who was my nurse, truly had to be, one
of God's angels sent from heaven up above.
And as she reached out her hand to me,
her eyes were filled with truest love.

She quietly told me not to worry, that
everything would be all right.
She gave me so much strength that I needed,
to make it thru the longest night.

For those were all the lonely hours, that I
must face, that never seemed to end.
Yes, in my fretful, painful moments, this
angel was so needed, my truest friend.

She brightened up my day for me, surrounding
me with sunshine's golden light.
A quiet reverence followed her, whenever
she came into my sight.

Her faith in God, she lived with everyday, as
she passed it on to everyone she met.
And thru all my many years of life, this
truest angel, I never will forget.

This loving, giving soul, wherever she may be,
with the beating of my heart, I surely know,
She is helping someone, somewhere, who is in need,
of that special faith, the truest love, that angel glow.

Written By Berniece Piercy

My Chance in Life

I don't want your pity,
If that's all you have to give,
It only makes me feel much worse,
And it doesn't help my chance to live.

My mountains may be higher,
But my heart is still the same,
Don't try to make me different,
As I struggle with life's game.

I want to be an equal.
To stand tall with all the best.
Because I must try harder,
Doesn't mean I can't pass the test.

So, just look straight into my eyes,
I need your help, your strength, your love.
I'm not asking for a fortune,
Or the moon up in the sky above.

By Berniece Piercy

Life's Great Lessons

Life just came crashing down on me, it was a
Rather stunning blow,
I really wasn't quite so smart, as I would
Try to show.

It really sets you thinking, when you fall right
On your face,
And some of life's great lessons, will surely put you
In your place.

I think I'll try now, once again, to make it right,
I'll start out slow,
And maybe if I'm very careful, my future will have a lot
To show.

In any case, if I'm to keep my balance in life's game,
I better make sure my mistakes, do not turn
Out to be just the same.

Written: 1980
By Berniece Piercy

Life

Can life be thus, as just the briefest stance?
To swiftly slip away, forgotten, to be ne'er more.
A shadow passing quickly thru the day and night of
time. Just searching ever, for a truly restful shore.

But, oh, life is so beautiful, so lovely, just to see.
And as real as the river, flowing quickly past.
With a touch as warm and soft as velvet's dawn. And
the greatest love, that brings much peace, at last.

Still, when the hour of parting, is so close at hand.
And the softest breeze, gently lulls each one to sleep.
There are tears, it is so hard to know, and try to understand.
With broken heart, and pain, that lies within, so deep.

And time, holds and keeps forever, all the golden memories.
In the book of life, so precious to behold.
Oh, dearest one, you gave to me, the sunshine bright.
For all eternity, as destiny, relives each story told.

Written By Berniece Piercy

Life's Tally

I don't know all the answers, nor do I claim I do.
For there is the old saying, "To thine own self be true."

I'll try to solve the problems, no matter what they be.
As some are very difficult, others simple, so I see.

I have to stop and think a while, try to figure every way.
And then things may go smoothly,
for the balance of the day.

No use to try and hurry, if it means making more mistakes.
Perfection really is my goal, no matter
how much work it takes.

And when the time will finally come,
for fame and all the glory,
I'll have to go back to the past, which tells the greatest story.

Be it rich or poor, success or strife, it
proves a point, that stands so true,
Whatever you put into life, life will
in turn, give back to you.

Written By
Berniece Piercy

Life's Disaster

When disaster strikes us, and it seems our lives are totally
Destroyed, and we are standing there in the devastation,
holding small treasures in our hands,
And still, somewhere in the ruins, and the ashes, there is a
tiny spark of our lives, that is left lying there,
We need to talk to God, we can have a new life, and replace
what we have lost, and God understands,

He loves us, He can give us strength, so we can believe in who
we really are, we can recover,
There is a new way to go, God is waiting to give us peace, and
His unending care, our lives are not over,

He will give us faith, and hold us in His arms, when we are
tired, a place to rest each weary head,
He will renew us, we need to close our eyes, and take the rest,
That He offers us, and not be filled with anxious thoughts
instead,

Tomorrow will start a new day, with a promise, and sunshine
everywhere,
This is our time to show how strong we really are, we need to
Give of our love, to everyone, and unite, for then we are doing
God's will,
All of our material things, that we have lost, can be replaced, and
now, we need to pray, and thank God, that no one has been
taken from us, and our loved ones are, close beside us, still.

Written 2009
By Berniece Piercy

I Do Not Walk Alone

I do not walk alone thru life, Jesus walks along with me,
He will take my hand to guide me, o'er the mountain trail,
    past the shining sea,

My strength is ever born anew, there is a quickness in my stride,
For His love can make the sunshine glow, in my pathway, and
    o'er the countryside,

Yes, my pain will go, and peace will come, and His gentle
    touch will calm my fears,
His words can ease my heartache, lift me up, and end my
    falling tears,

Life can make us tired and weary, and the burdens bend us low,
There is no way to make it, without Jesus, to lead us e'er we go,

I can smile and share my gladness, care for the sick, and help
    the poor,
For I do not walk alone thru life, Jesus is there to tend me,
    forevermore.

Written
1970
By Berniece Piercy

God's Gift of Love

Borrowed for a little while, my life, my joy, my love,
A precious gift to nurture, from our loving Jesus, up above,

My dearest child, I never knew that holding you, could make
my heart so glad,
Or that losing you forevermore, could make my days and
nights, so sad,

Oh, God, please give me strength enough, to stand tall, and
go on with my life, each day,
Altho, tomorrow seems so far away, so unreal, with the pain
that I must bear,
And the mountains ahead of me, will seem much higher, as
I go along my way,

And thank you, God, for giving me this adorable child, for
these passed treasured years,
I know now, that He was always yours, amid the days and
nights, of endless tears,

And some day on the other side, I will hold my child, so close
to me, once more,
And I will give my child, all my love, as God welcomes me to
heaven's shore.

Written
1983
By Berniece Piercy

God's Grace For Us

By the grace of God, we awaken every coming day,
To embrace the blessings that he has to give to all.
Every waking moment will be rewarding,
If we so desire to know his gifts, both large and small.

There is no door in front of us to block our view.
We make the decisions, and the choices are our very own.
But with God beside us, we can choose with wisdom.
And the castles that we build, will
not come tumbling down.

God put us here to grow, and love each other, this we know.
To bring peace, and give hope to all,
who have lost their way.
So gather close, While the power of God unites us.
As we all listen to the truthful words he has to say.

Written By
Berniece Piercy
2007

God's Faith Will Prevail

Our faith in God, is being tested every passing day,
Sometimes, it seems like the answers
that we seek, may not be there,
But miracles are waiting, they will happen in our lifetime,
We must keep our faith, for God's truest
love is waiting everywhere.

We need to thank him, that there can be a new beginning,
In each brand new day that blossoms in the morning's light,
As we pray and our strength is renewed, we will recover,
Loving hands will reach out to us,
to help us, to make it right.

The darkness is always waiting to enclose us,
But God's sunshine will overcome, and
we will see the light again,
God's faith has been there always, tho
tried and tested, it still prevails,
We can trust in God who loves us, and our
lives will not have been lived in vain.

By Berniece Piercy

God's Tomorrow

Sometimes there are no answers,
As we trod life's daily way,
For mountains loom ahead of us,
And clouds will block the sunshine's ray.

But thru it all the beauty of the sun,
Will always shine so bright.
And the lovely golden moonbeams,
Will light a lonely, darkest night.

God's hand will touch us lightly,
To steady us, to make us strong,
For his strength will always be there,
At dawn's break, and thru the hours so long.

He will bless us and sustain us,
Give us peace and faith each day,
Renew our hope for each tomorrow,
And in our lives, his love will always stay.

By Berniece Piercy

Grandpa

Grandpa has a brand new baby boy, who has such beautiful
    eyes of blue,
Grandpa is so very proud of him, yes, this grandson will smile
    at Grandpa, very quickly, it is true,

One day this little boy will reach for Grandpa's hand, they
    will know there are so many adventures for them to find,
With upturned face, and trust, and so much love to give,
One thing is for sure, he will always be in his Grandpa's mind,

Sometimes Grandpa's eyes will fill with tears, his heart is full,
    for this child has captured him so,
Until each man becomes a Grandpa, too, this added beauty
    to their lives, they will never know,

And someday, this Grandson will grow up, and look back to
    his Grandpa's knowing ways,
All the stories and beautiful times they shared together, so
    much love and understanding, that will bring a smile
These dearest memories will last him, the rest of his days.

By Berniece Piercy

Farther Away From Jesus

The whole world is getting farther away from Jesus,
When only darkness fills so many lives, each passing day.
When they cannot see the sunshine's
beauty that is all around them,
Cannot shed the burdens of the daily
strife, that comes their way.

When they have forgotten how to sing the words of Jesus,
In the songs that filled their lives with joy, so long ago,
As they stumble thru each waking hour with weakness,
Whatever happened to that little girl
or boy, that we used to know?

Oh, dear Jesus, now it seems that they are really lost,
They are your children and they cannot find their way,
Please reach for them, and please light their paths tonight,
If you can hold them close to you for
a little while, dear Lord.
They can rest their weary heads, find peace
and love, and their lives may be all right.

Written by Berniece Piercy
2000

Freedom's Worth

Freedom is the right to speak the words we want to say,
Freedom is the chance to make a
choice each brand new day.
Freedom keeps away the chains that
would bind our every move,
Freedom is the message given by our flag that flies above.

Sometimes we take for granted the smallest ordinary things,
Perhaps forgetting to be thankful, for
the blessings each day brings.
But we best not let the memories of
the heartache and the pain,
Fade from our minds so easily, for it
could happen once again.

Be proud to be an American, no matter what the daily cost,
Stand firm behind our country, let not our
freedom be taken, and forever lost.
And when our country's anthem rings
out to us, so loud and clear,
Just think about the meaning of the
words of freedom that you hear.

For its true, there just no other country,
that has so much to give,
God bless this land, "America", this land
of freedom, is where we live.

By Berniece Piercy

Friendship

Friendship can't be measured, as a moment swiftly passed.
It is meant to last forever, tho trodden
on, and much harassed.

There are many times when friendship
fills our days and longest nights.
A friend so strong to lean on, who will
help us stand up for our rights.

A friend will forever listen, to all the words we have to say.
Then understand, and try to help, in a quiet, gentle way.

Friendship in our lifetime, has to pass the greatest test.
And when the worst is over, still be shining, at it's best.

So if now, in your lifetime, you are
someone's friend in need,
You are a ray of sunshine, a truly greatest soul, indeed.

You have given hope anew, and faith restored, once more,
You know you'll stay right to the end, because
that's what truest friends are for.

A friend will dry our teardrops, and take away the fears.
And they will always be there, to lead
us, thru the many years.

Berniece Piercy

Eighty Great Years

Who would have ever thought, that we all would be standing
    here, today,
Looking at young and old pictures, and we still can't believe
That eighty years have come to us, as we have traveled on
    life's way,

We all have to look back and say, "It was a great trip, to get
    to where we are,
We climbed some pretty tall mountains, as we struggled at times,
To get to the top, and try to reach that special star,

And God was walking along right beside us, to pick us up, if
    we should fall,
And the greatest part of being old is, most of the time, we will
    remember it all,

All of the treasured yesterdays, that are now gone, will always
    be close to our hearts, it's true,
They could never be replaced, there was so much of life to
    live for me and you,

We have seen sunshine, and dark clouds, and laughter, and
    sometimes tears,
We were surrounded by our beautiful families, the dearest ones,
Who were always there for us to have and hold, thru all the
    passing years,

So we will keep looking forward to as many years as God will
    give us, you know,
For life still holds much beauty, the new dawnings, the
    sunsets, and more,
In spite of all the aches and pains and everything else, we plan
    to stay and enjoy as much as we can, before we go,

And to get right down to the closing lines, we are still moving
Along pretty well, and you know we surely, dearly loved it all,
And our book of life's pages has many golden memories, that
    we can always recall.

Sept, 2009
Berniece Piercy

Challenging The Sea

The rise and fall of this failing ship, the waves
matching each move Throughout the night, the
relentless strikes of lightening above, it's so Unlikely
this ship will see the shore in its flight.

The merciless sea, and the gusting wind, the pounding
of the waves Against the hull, seems this endless fight
will never end, and suddenly The battle is won, and
the sea is spent, and finally there is a peaceful lull.

The crewman were soaked, and tired from their
plight, giving all of the strength they had to give,
God's blessings were with them, It's true, And when
the task was over they gave thanks to God, who
did strengthen them in their struggle to live.

By Berniece Piercy
Written Feb. 2004

Believe In Yourself

Believe in yourself, for God has made you into perfection,
Do not doubt the power, that God gives to you, everyday,
The world is so complex, in many of the things, that we all try,
We have been watching all of our dreams, and they always
  seem to slip away,

Believe in yourself, for you are your own best critic, you have
To like what you see, in the mirror, because that is all there
  is, for now,
God gave you, your own talents to work with, so get busy, you
  have work to do, you will make it to the top, somehow,

You need to look for your best qualities, and go forward with
  them,
Just stand tall, for whatever happens, you are a child of God,
  it is true,
He wants you to dream big dreams, and move ahead, love
  yourself, because God loves you, and believes in you,

Tell yourself life will get better, live in faith, and stay hopeful,
  as you awaken to each tomorrow,
Your greatness is within yourself, what is truly in your heart?
You will succeed, God has much faith for you, and unending
  strength, that you can borrow.

Written in 2007
By Berniece Piercy

Alone With God

Today, as I sit alone with God, who is always by my side,
See His creative beauty, reaching far across the earth so wide,
As I watch the flowing river, or see a lovely bird in flight,
I know I need such peace and joy, to keep my life forever right,

I need the brightest sunshine, and the rain upon my face,
A cooling breeze on a summer day, and the helping hand of
      God's true grace,

I can hear the faintest whisper, of the leaves in autumn's stay,
And when the woods are so quiet and snowy white on a lovely
      winter's day,

I need the tiny rosebud, so innocent and pure, with springtime's
      crimson beauty, thru all the years it will endure,

I see the moonlight, soft and velvet, and the diamond stars
      above, yesterday, today, and forever, these are the surest
      signs of God's great love.

Berniece G. Piercy

America

We all love America, it will always be our country,
Where we will have the right to choose, what we will do.
Still, sometimes we never stop and think about it,
We take for granted, every passing day, it's true.

Our heritage, the freedom, that was always there,
Guarded and protected by the brave ones we love.
Who fought, or died, or always kept a lonely vigil,
To keep our flag of freedom, forever, flying up above.

How our hearts would break, if
suddenly the hour would come.
When no longer would we have the right to liberty,
And we could not speak, or move without restrictions.
And slowly, surely, life would end for you and me.

We must look beyond the scene that is before us,
We must give thanks for all the blessings that we know.
And we must believe in peace and love for all mankind,
And be proud to be Americans, then America will grow.

Written By Berniece Piercy
1984

Asking God

Have you ever thought about just asking God?,
What to do, when life is a battle from morning until night.
We run around and blindly rush ahead, each day,
Until we are burned out, and everything
in our lives is still not right.

Look up to the heavens, all our answers are with God,
We are forever spinning our wheels, and going nowhere fast,
Ask God, Let him help you find the best way to go,
And then tomorrow, the sun will shine brightly, at last.

It isn't so hard to talk to God, you know,
He loves us, and our burdens, He will understand,
He knows our lives are not easy, as we
struggle to survive once more,
So today, just reach up, and ask God to take your hand.

Written By
Berniece Piercy
2007

God Is Listening

God does grant our wishes as we live out every day,
For we are blessed in many ways an
answer to the times we pray.
Believing, and to ever hope, and our faith to always keep,
Yes, God will add some peace and love, when
mountains to be climbed are steep.

As we help others try in life, so shall we reap and gain,
For many are the weary souls, so lonely,
and so filled with pain.
They need the brightest sunshine, with
the warmth and lovely glow,
They need the strength we give them,
and the kindness that we show.

For we have much that they have not,
our growing riches so complete,
And many struggle endlessly, to live
each day that they must meet.
Yes, we really can be thankful, when
we see our loved ones near,
For God is always listening, and our
prayers he will always hear.

By Berniece Piercy

A Battle That Can't Be Won

When the flaming swords of battle, are falling
to the earth, and some of the bitter hatred
pours out upon the ground, so all in vain,

What has each army, so devoted to winning, really
won so far? We watch all of the love, and goodness of
mankind, as it is so easily, without mercy, slain.

Cold hearts that will never beat with love, eyes
streaked with madness, and hair all flying wild,

Where is the compassion that holds this
world together? Can this forever defiant one,
still be known as God's loving child?

Let all men put aside their weapons of war, For all the riches
and land, that is won will never hold true. And the tears of
man, will surely fall like rain, when they take the time, and
finally see the horror, that man at war can do, perhaps man
will fall down to his knees, and ask God's forgiveness then

But it may be too late to save it all, as history repeats itself
again, and yes, again,
We really don't see a happy winner thru all the years gone by,
that we can recall.

By Berniece Piercy
Written 2006

Destiny

We wander to the edge of time, where silence is the king,
We slip and slide, are never sure, of a solitary thing.

We know that we are moving, as the wind, that starts to blow,
Sometimes a whirlwind sailing high, and other times, with
    movement slow,

Like a ship that rolls from side to side, and plows the sea so deep,
Thus stirs the depth and quiet, where so many treasures sleep,

With journey spent, and over, and gone the ocean's roar,
All ships must surely make their way, again, back to the shore,

For wherever we started, when life's first breathe began,
We will again come home to stay, within our lifetime span.

No matter all the sights we've seen, or gold and riches we
    have claimed,
Fantastic places we have been, or for goals in life, that we
    have aimed.

Time is waiting silently, it has traced our paths so clear,
And brought us to our knees once more, passing so quickly,
    ever we fear.

And we have not reached that mountain top, or lived or loved
    our best,
We have missed much beauty in our lives, we haven't passed
    the greatest test,

And panic fills our heart so full, to know life's chance seems
   to be spent,
Our mind fills quickly thru the days, with lovely memories
   time has lent.

No one can understand or even know, the feelings of the heart,
We would love to live our lives once more, and go back to
   the very start.

Perhaps we would change so many things, or even go a
   different way,
But chances are, life's greatest deeds, have formed a pattern,
   meant to stay.

So, we should search for peace, for it is there, and we should
   see all the beauty, too,
And fill our lives with so much love, then life will truly seem
   brand new.

Written 1970
Berniece G. Piercy

The Greatest Need

I was praying for a miracle, that only God can give,
A happening that is so rare, to see in all the days we live.

I was praying for a miracle, I surely needed one,
I had to face reality, and it seemed all hope was gone.

For all miracles, as we do know, do come from heaven above,
For God alone has the power, and the strength, of all His love.

There is no living mortal, that can make this be all right,
Perhaps there will be an answer, to my prayers in the night,

There are the saddest moments, and my eyes will fill with tears,
I have the feeling of great loss, thru the passing of the years,

I gaze up to the sky, where there is heaven's peaceful shore,
And again I'll pray so silently, for a miracle, once more.

Written
1970
By Berniece Piercy

God's Presence

On eagle's wings I'll mount the sky, where breezes so cool,
Will touch my face,
God's presence will be so close to me, his love will fill this
Heavenly place.

Life is very fragile, and sometimes
gone, before we can even try,
This life, god's gift, is truly precious, not ours to waste, or
just sit idly by.

Oh, god, the beauty that you have made, the mountains, the
valleys, the oceans so blue,
Cool forests and the sunshine to warm us each day,
your artistic show in colors, so glorious and true.

Dear god, your strength will hold us
together, tho the clouds are
never far away,
Yes, we will fly, as eagles, and touch a silver star,
And god will not let us fall; he will
tend us, in his own loving way.

Berniece Piercy
Written 2006

My Dearest One

The day is slowly ending now, and night is drawing near.
Without thinking, I just turned to call your name.
Then suddenly I realize, that there is no one here but me.
And I know that life has changed,
and it can never be the same.

It that only hours ago, you were here, right by my side.
And now, this moment, I can feel your
presence ever close to me.
There was a familiar pattern, as each day was born to end.
We just took life for granted, things were as they should be.

So much of time had slipped away,
and we were growing older.
Is it possible all those years were really gone?
Why, it seems like only yesterday,
that into my life, you came.
Now sadness overcomes me, for I know that I am all alone.

So many hours are mirrored in the corners of my heart.
Countless memories of youth and love that I have kept.
All of these treasures will stay, they
will be mine, forevermore.
So many thoughts can bring a smile, still
others, know the tears, that I have wept.

Just give your hand, unto my own,
So that I can lean on you,
You'll make my days, my weeks, my years,
The happiest time, my whole life thru.

By Berniece Piercy

Angels Of Mercy

The angels of mercy, dressed all in white,
Tending the sick through the day and night.
Never having a free moment, as each call they would heed,
Hurrying on their way to the next one in need.

Angels of mercy, they will always be near,
To hold someone's hand or wipe away a fallen tear.
Each will never tire; God will strengthen them anew.
He will bless them and them in all that they do.

From the morning's first light of dawn,
The stars at night shine brightly above.
They will always be there, unfailing,
Still, with a nurse's kind and gentle love.

The vigil is very long, and many tasks never end.
But though weary, they will be the patient's best friend.
They will make someone happy with a kind word or smile,
Devoted to their work, going that extra mile.

When it is time to go home, and their
work is done for the day,
Hoping that they have not forgotten anyone on their way.
So the sick need not worry, there is
much kindness and loving care,
For the beautiful angels of mercy will always be there.

Written By
Berniece Piercy

Call To War

We are sending all the young boys, they
have to leave and go to war,
Hardly more than children, going away to other lands so far.

This hell of kill or be killed, that
haunts them night and day,
This is no game, this massacre, this
is the horror of war's way.

To have, so many years ago, the greatest
blessing of a brand new son,
With no thoughts about the battles, the
wars, that some day must be won.

The memories of tiny children, gentle,
growing with each passing year,
Cowboys and Indians, and guns to tote,
childhood friends that were always near.

That boyish grin and eyes so bright, just
reaching out for all our love,
The closeness of a family, too, and the
strong belief of God above.

But now, they can never in their lifetime,
be just little boys again,
Friends have died, and they have been in the
cold, and filled with fear and pain.

Now, my son, you have met the task, come,
and sit awhile, and quietly just rest,
You have given everything, you fought in
the war, and did your very best.

Perhaps someday, somehow, in our lifespan,
all men will learn to love each other,
And they will never have to kill again, for
each man they meet, he is a brother.

By Berniece Piercy

Forgiveness

God wants us all to forgive each other
now, the passing years of
heartache and sadness, have already came and are gone.

There were many tears and family
isolations, where our loved ones
have been left, so all alone.

Brothers, sisters, moms, and dads, all
of the families, open up your
hearts, and find a loved one now, today.

We all started out together in the
beginning, we know, there was love,
and we did it all God's way.

Those later years are quickly coming
to a close, Don't waste the
treasured time that is left.

Love has been lost, with all the bitterness,
and maybe, even hate.

Just run and hug each other, and say,
"I love you. Please forgive me.",
Before it is too late.

Find someone that you have left behind,
because of a lifestyle, that
caused a rift.

God always teaches us to have forgiveness,
that is one of his greatest
loving gifts.

Put love back into the families, there
will be goodness in your heart,
and it won't cost you anything.

Renew the love that once was there,
Think of all the blessings it will
bring.

Time is short, we're not sure of tomorrow,
hearts have been badly
broken, through all the years.

The tears that have fallen from so much
sadness, can be replaced with
the precious "Forgiveness Tears"

Written by Berniece Piercy
Sept. 2000

Polish boy

I wish I could help you,
As I see you there trembling in fear.
It seems like there is nothing I can do,
I start to see your eyes fill with tears.

I am thinking, why does it have to be you?
I just want to take your place.
I know what the guard is going to do,
He keeps looking at your horrified face.

I want you to know I am praying,
I just want you to be strong.
Can you hear the hateful words the guard is saying?
I can tell this painful day will be long.

By: Brittany Swiger

Printed in the United States
By Bookmasters